Selling With Honor

Jody N Holland

ISBN: 0983983593
ISBN-13: 978-0-9839835-9-0

DEDICATION

This book is dedicated to the countless professionals who
are helping prospects, clients, and customers to find the
solutions that they need in order to run their businesses
more effectively and live their lives more fully.

CONTENTS

ACKNOWLEDGMENTS

I would like to acknowledge my father-in-law, who may not realize it, but is an amazing salesperson. He is an incredible fund-raiser, persuader, and leader!

I would like to acknowledge the self-help industry for continuing to inspire me to be more, do more, and have more than I had yesterday.

THE BEGINNING
CALM BELIEF

Selling With Honor is based on applying the Bushido Code to sales and is a series of seven principles for selling who you are, what you offer, and the solutions that you provide. I am fascinated by the application of the Bushido to today's world, especially the Warrior's Way of Selling. The blend of complete calm, absolute focus, and incredible discipline are what are needed for today's salesperson to be truly successful and to bring honor to their employer.

Calm is something that is not often seen in this world. In the age of always on, always going, and over-stimulation, it is a stretch to find quiet in our world or in our mind. To be calm means to be still, quiet, and tranquil. I believe that this is one of the great challenges to finding fulfillment in life. People are continuously judging themselves against everyone and everything around them. They are trying to define themselves by the things that they have and the status that they have achieved. The interesting paradox that seems to recur is that when we define ourselves by the things that we have, then we will always need more things. People seem to believe that if they can simply acquire a few more things, then their life will be complete. In the movie, "Fight Club," after the main character, played by actor Edward Norton, has just lost his condo to an explosion, he explains to Tyler Derden, played by Brad Pitt, that he had put together the perfect collection of furniture. He had the sofa that he had always wanted. He says that no matter what else happened, he knew that the sofa was taken care of. The violence in this movie is a backdrop to the struggle that existed between a young generation and corporate culture that was selling people things that still did not create calm in their lives. The part that really hits home is that of people buying things that they don't need to try and find a way to calm themselves. Being calm means that one is centered. They are able to let go of the noise in life and simply be. There are different ways to achieve this calm. For some, the calm is achieved through exercise. For others, it is achieved through meditation. For still others, it is achieved by doing what their passion is, whether that be art, writing, study, or anything that is a true extension of themselves. In order to identify what calm feels like, take 24 hours and turn off all electronics, including your phones, TV, computers, radio, or anything else that produces noise or consumes electricity. Get away from everything and focus on the quiet that exists. If you will do this, you will catch a glimpse of what calm is supposed to feel like. It takes time and practice to achieve this, though. It is not the norm for this world. Once you have achieved calm, you are ready to gain focus.

Absolute focus is the state in which all obstacles fade from existence. When I was first learning to break boards in martial arts, it was learning that the board did not even exist. There are so many opportunities to fail in this world. They are around every corner, in every challenge, and engrained into the psyche of humanity. They are always there if... that is what you focus on. Conversely, there are so many opportunities to win in this world. They are in every step that we take, every breath that gives life, every growth opportunity that we are given, every call we make, every presentation, everything that we do. The difference between seeing the success or the failure is simply what our focus is locked on to. Are we focused on the challenge or are we focused on the end goal? My sensei taught me to see beyond the challenge while still acknowledging its existence. The board was there. It was there, though, to ensure that I truly desired to go beyond it. When I kept my focus on 8 inches past the board, the board simply snapped

and yielded to my desires. Absolute focus in business
is the same way. When we are able to consistently
focus beyond the obstacle, that obstacle will always
yield to our desires. It will simply fall out of the way
so that we can succeed in the way that we desire to
succeed. When we have calmed our mind and focused
on the exact end desire that we have, then we
naturally flow into absolute discipline.

Discipline is the art of doing what we must so that we
can achieve what we desire. Discipline is the process
of creating order and structure. People who avoid
discipline are avoiding systematic success. The
mistake that people make in their minds is to believe
that discipline is a punishment, especially when it is
self-discipline. Discipline is the ordering of our mind
to align what we truly desire with the behaviors that
get us to that end result. For example, if you desired
to lose 10 pounds, would you know what people who
weighed less than you do? Do they eat differently
than you do? Do they exercise differently than you
do? If the answer is yes, then you know what their
behaviors are and what results those behaviors create.
This means that you have the knowledge to get to
that end result if that is what you desire to do. You
simply have to choose to do the same things that
others have done. When you choose to follow a
specific path toward success, you will have become a
disciple of success. To follow that path means that
you get that result. People spend too much time

complicating the sales process with 20 techniques to close a prospect and 10 cold calling techniques and the like. It isn't that these things are bad. It is simply that none of them works without the right beliefs in place, without the right discipline to get you to that desired end. If you knew that there were four things that you must do on a daily basis in order to be successful, would you do them? If you knew that you simply had to behave in the right way for 3 hours per day in order to be financially successful, would you? If you answered yes and you honestly will commit to discipline yourself for success, then you will be able to attain what others will not. The choice to make your success more important than your other activities will create the discipline that you need to win. Choose what you will do. Choose what you will be.

Each of these things works together to weave the fabric of your belief system. Contrary to what you learned in elementary school, you are not what you eat. You are what you believe. Your actions will always flow out of your beliefs. You will justify your thoughts and your actions because they are the reflection of what you believe at your core. If your belief is that you are a bad salesperson or that your product is not worth buying, this will be reflected in your daily actions. If your belief is that your product or service is incredible and must be shared with the world, then you will not be able to stop yourself.

One of the reasons that network marketing companies have done so well is that they have understood how to create belief in others. In an event in Atlanta, Georgia, in 2013, the theme for this women's organization was "Believe." They spent a great deal of time talking about what these women believed about life, and family, and success. They drew their desires out of them and helped them to focus intently on what they believed was possible and what they believed was their role in creating a better life for themselves and their family. It is the belief that drives a person to action. The following formula is the way in which each of us creates our world around us.

Belief
- This product is incredible!
- Everyone deserves the chance to try this!

Thoughts
- I need to share this.
- I want to talk about my passion every chance I get!

Actions
- I tell my story about how this product helps.
- I talk about how my life is different because of this product.

Result
- People are excited to learn more.
- People are happy to buy from me and love their purchase.

As you go through from beliefs, to thoughts, to actions, to results, it becomes apparent that it is the foundation of your beliefs that will always create the results that you get in life. Those results will either reinforce your beliefs or modify them. Your results are the experiences that you have. Never forget the importance of those experiences. They are what shape a person. Beliefs work in both directions, though. If you believe, for example, that nothing good ever happens to you, then you will think about the bad things that could and should happen to you. You will take action on things that will end up leading to a negative result. This negative result will reinforce your belief that nothing good ever happens to you, and the cycle will continue. We cannot change our lives by changing only our actions. We must discover what our beliefs are and change those at the core. As Henry Ford once said, "The man who thinks he can and the man who thinks he can't, are both correct." Which will it be for you? What will you choose to believe? Will you seek out a product or service that you believe the entire world needs to hear about or will you find something that you sort of believe in? The stronger your belief, the larger your victory. To live with honor and sell with honor, you must absolutely believe that what you are offering is honorable.

Take a few moments and write out why the product or service that you represent is beneficial to people, or organizations, or whoever your end user might be. Don't just write out the features and benefits. Write out the way that your product will make the end user feel and how they will be a better person, or a better organization as a result of using this product/service.

_____

_____

_____

_____

_____

_____

_____

_____

_____

_____

_____

_____

_____

_____

_____

CHAPTER 1
THE 1ST VIRTUE - RIGHTEOUSNESS

The first Virtue of Bushido is Rectitude, also known as Righteousness. This virtue indicates that a person has lived their life in such a way that all of their actions are justified and they could be judged as having done what was right in every situation. This is quite a task for anyone to try to achieve. From a salesperson's perspective, in order to be judged as having lived your work life in a way that would be pleasing to those whom you serve, you would have to honor your boss, your customers, and your coworkers with your actions. As you begin looking at the meaning of being a righteous salesperson, it would follow that these actions and attitudes would be absolutes...

1. One must put forth their best effort from the start to the finish of every work day.

The challenge that most people have in putting forth their best effort is that they are unsure of what that actually means. Albert Einstein said, "If we did all that we are capable of, we would literally astound ourselves." Your best effort will require you to be focused on the things that bring results on a daily basis and will require you to strip away the things that limit your success. You must have a system for managing what you put into your day and what you give your attention to each day. In sales, there are only a few things that bring your best results. Things like connecting with people, discovering their needs, offering a solution based on your product or service, and implementing that solution are among the top daily activities of the fully productive sales person. If you attack each day with the focus of bringing in new business, you will find your success. Your goal cannot be to make calls. Your goal has to be to be fully immersed in your product or service with the intent of bringing success to a new client every day through what you offer. Take a serious look, an honest look, at what you do during the day. Are you honoring your employer by giving your very best effort? Do you put in a full day's work to find success? Or do you spend a great deal of time with the miscellaneous things that do not increase the business? If you are not fully engaged in increasing the business of the company, you are not living a righteous life. If you are giving your full eight hours to connecting, discovering, solving, and implementing, each and every day, then you are living a righteous life as a sales warrior. Which is it for you?

2. One must identify the best solution for the client, even if that is a solution that is not provided by your company.

This can be tough for some people because salespeople often go in with a preconceived notion of what they intend to sell. If you are not listening to your prospect, you will simply try to sell them what you have instead of what they need. The majority of the time, you will have something that will help the client. However, there are times that your solution is not the right one and the client should be directed to a better option that fits their needs. An example of this would be what I have seen in the automobile industry. There is story after story about how a person will go in with a specific need for a certain car and the salesperson will just keep trying to redirect them to the car that they want the customer to buy instead of the car that is right for the customer. One such story was when an associate of mine went into a Chevrolet Dealership and wanted to look at a new Tahoe. They had two children and were beginning to haul sports equipment around and wanted a vehicle that would be comfortable on long trips. Several of their friends had the same vehicle and were very satisfied with it. The salesperson had gotten excited about the Avalanche, that had just come out the year before. As my friend asked questions about the Tahoe, the salesperson just kept redirecting them and saying the features and benefits of the other vehicle. The salesperson was NOT listening to the needs or desires of the customer. They simply wanted to sell an Avalanche. There may have been a bonus for selling them that month or the salesperson could have just liked that vehicle. Either way, after 45 minutes of trying to get information about the vehicle that they wanted and after reluctantly taking a test drive in a vehicle that they were not interested in, the Avalanche, my friend told the salesperson that they had decided not to buy a vehicle at all at this point. They left the dealership and went to a completely different brand, Ford. When we don't listen to our customer and focus on serving them the best way that we can, we are not living a righteous life. We are not doing what is best for the customer. The Sales Warrior will always focus on what the needs and desires of the customer are, over their own desires.

3. One must focus at all times on bringing success to their employer.

Success is not measured solely with finances. Success is measured by honor, reputation, and results. When a person is focused on bringing success to their employer, they are focused on building the kind of reputation that attracts more customers to the employer and lifts them up to a place of honor among their peers. The world seems to have forgotten that when an opportunity arises to find success with an employer, the duty to seize that opportunity rests with the employees, contractors, etc. The job of the employer is to create the opportunity. The job of the sales warrior is to step boldly onto the field of battle and claim victory after victory. If your focus, as a sales warrior, is to make your employer successful and wealthy, then you will find the same for yourself. The universe will bring you what you desire for others. We are all connected. If you desire ill for your employer, ill will be given to you. If you desire success for your employer, success will be given to you. You must focus on the success of everyone around you, especially the organization or person that has given you an opportunity. They desire for you to be successful, to seize the opportunity that is before you. Your job is to do all that is in your power, each and every day, to bring honor and success to your employer.

4. One must work to bring success to their coworkers and assist them in their personal and business growth.

What you send out will return to you. If you send out hate and distrust, then you will get hate and distrust in return. If you send out joy and success, then joy and success will return to you. When you joyfully help the other people in your organization find their success, they will do the same for you. Even though you will encounter some people who will initially try to take advantage of your kindness and not intend to return it to you, it is the kindness that you create that comes back from others that counts. Most of these people will come around. Others will be recognized for their selfishness by the employer and will move on to other places. It isn't what others do that you should be worried about or focused on. It is what you do that is your concern. Do not wait for someone else to live with righteousness before you do the same. Set the example in caring for your coworkers, sharing insights that you have learned, helping them close deals, and collaborating for their success and the enhanced success of your employer.

5. One must end each day knowing that they put in the greatest effort that they were capable of giving.

A righteous warrior sleeps well at night with the knowledge that they have done all that they were capable of doing to find success. At the end of each day, take some time to write out what you accomplished.

In brief, to be righteous means that you must be all that you are capable of and nothing less. You may not slack or become lazy or give only a partial effort.

This is the way of the Sales Warrior!

What is it that you are capable of being? If you knew you would not and could not fail, what would you do?

_____

_____

_____

_____

_____

_____

_____

_____

_____

_____

_____

_____

_____

_____

_____

_____

_____

_____

_____

_____

_____

_____

_____

_____

_____

_____

_____

_____

_____

CHAPTER 2
THE 2ND VIRTUE – RESPECT

The second virtue of the Sales Warrior is that of respect. A warrior is respectful of their customers, their coworkers, their leaders, and their competitors. There is never a reason to bash one's competition. They watch the things that they say and are considered to be master's of their tongue. They do not use foul language, make derogatory statements about others, or speak ill of those who compete with them in their chosen arena. Their respect for others is not given as a result of others first respecting them. They respect all people around them because that is what is right and it requires no reciprocation for its survival.

The term, respect, originally meant "to have regard

for, without judgment." The Samurai had respect for anyone and everyone that they did battle with. It was an honor to live in their chosen profession. Try to imagine being alive during the time of the Samurai. Any time that you would step onto the field of battle, you would assume that your competitor was worthy and you would be honored to do battle with them. To respect another warrior was to respect one's self. Without respecting others, one cannot respect one's self.

One of the great challenges that salespeople often fail at is showing respect for everyone with whom they come into contact. I had a sales manager who told me once that he loved to take people's money. He felt like he owned their soul when he got them to spend more than they should and at times more than they really could. I remember looking at him and wondering how he could look at himself in the mirror and see someone whom he should respect. To respect a customer is to desire the best fit for them. It is to focus on finding a solution that is right for them and will bring them success and fulfillment. Respect for the customer is to always focus on how you can help them to achieve their objectives, how you can honor them with your service. They respect and honor your business when they are confident that you have their best interests at heart.

This goes beyond our interactions with our

customers, though. We must look at all areas of our lives and evaluate how we are interacting with others. Every interaction that we have with another person will leave them either better or worse. It never leaves them the same as they were before. This all begins with your thought-life, though. It begins with the way that you look at others. What do you see when you look at your coworkers? Do you see their value or do you see the worst in them? When we keep our focus on the good that others have to offer, then we are respecting the best of who they are. When we do this, then the best parts of us will be illuminated in the minds of others. Respect begins with our thoughts and is translated into our actions and behaviors. If you wish to see what your thoughts have been, look at what your behaviors have been and evaluate them as an outside observer looking in. What are you doing to demonstrate respect?

We respect our coworkers and bosses by giving all of ourselves to the task. If you are not getting the highest result that you are capable of, then you are not demonstrating respect. One of the struggles that I have continually heard about from employers is that of employees not giving their all to the task. Employers and employees often appear to be in a stand-off, waiting for the other one to improve and give their best. Both sides seem to be saying that they will work hard and be respectful once, and only once, the other side does something incredible. When we are respectful, it is not as a condition of another person's behavior. Each and every day, we should wake up and strive to make a difference by being the highest version of ourselves that exists. Every task that we are honored with, we should strive to give everything that we have to it. It is once we give our all, that others feel, see, and know that we are truly respectful.

We discipline ourselves daily to hone our art and to bring success to our company. This discipline is accomplished by outlining the things that make the greatest difference to the success of the company and to ourselves. We then do the things that bring success to the company before we do anything else. In sales, there are five things that must be done daily as a discipline in order to bring success to our employer and to ourselves.

We must...

1. Connect with others who could benefit from what we have to offer.

2. Discover what their needs are.

3. Find the right solution for the customer/client.

4. Implement the solution.

5. Ask for a referral so we might help others as

well.

These five items will be discussed more in-depth in the second half of the book, but keep them in mind as you continue to learn and absorb this information. It is self-discipline that matters. It is your ability to do what is necessary every single day that will make the most incredible difference to you and your career. The respectful salesperson is not waiting for someone else to do something for them. They are not waiting for another brochure or another marketing push. They are men and women of actions. It is in our actions that we demonstrate our thoughts and beliefs.

The Sales Warrior speaks only good of those with whom and for whom they work. Our world would be a much more engaging place if our focus was on how we could respect others instead of on how we could slam them. As an exercise, I would challenge you to spend seven consecutive days thinking and saying only good things about others. In fact, think only positive thoughts for seven continuous days. If you mess up and think something negative, simply start over at that exact moment. This includes everyone in your life, even those that don't respect you. Respect others in both thought and action.

Respect even those that are attempting to do battle directly with you. Respect them as you would respect a friend. We respect our competitors by acknowledging that our customer has the right to purchase from whomever can best fill their needs. When we keep this in mind, we strive to be the best version of ourselves and to represent the best version of our company. We focus on the needs of the customer above the needs of our company or ourselves.

If our competition speaks ill of us, we do not speak ill of them. What we want for another is what we want for ourselves. We are all connected. You cannot wish harm on another without wishing harm on a part of yourself. The energy that binds us together impacts us with every thought that we think and every action that we take. Watch your beliefs about others, for they are the thoughts that you think and will manifest in the actions that you take. When you take a negative or derogatory approach, even to your competitors, you are taking a negative approach to yourself.

If our customer has bought from a competitor, we acknowledge that they made the best choice they could make with the information that they had. Our job as a sales warrior is to uncover what they have, what they desire, and what is missing. When we discover what is missing that will bring greater success to our client, we are able to move them forward. Do not simply tell your prospect that you are better and the competition is bad. When we bash our competition, we are saying to our client, "You are not smart and were not smart for making the choice that you made." I don't know any leaders with self-respect that will respond positively to that. If we bash our competition as a choice by our prospect, we are bashing the prospect. When we bash our prospect, we are bashing our own chances of serving the prospect as a client. We are, therefore, bashing ourselves and our chances of success. Show respect for everyone. That must be your primary objective.

If our objective is to show respect, others will also respect us. If we choose not to show respect, we are inviting disrespect. Be the warrior who can demonstrate respect in everything that they do. Read the following affirmation every morning for the next 21 mornings. Read it before you leave the house as a way of planning how you will interact with others.

I will respect those around me.

I know that I must respect myself in order to respect others.

I know that not respecting others is a sign that I do not have respect for myself.

I do respect myself.

I do respect my customers.

I do respect my coworkers and bosses.

I do respect my competition.

I will live a life of virtue!

Write out three to five ways that you can demonstrate respect for others. What actions or behaviors will be interpreted as respectful? Write these out and then choose to do them every day!

1. _____

   _____

   _____

2. _____

   _____

   _____

3. _____

   _____

   _____

4. _____

_____

_____

5. _____

_____

_____

CHAPTER 3
THE 3RD VIRTUE – HEROIC COURAGE

Hiding like a turtle inside of its shell is no way to live. We were not meant to be the kind of people that hid from struggle or ran from challenges. It does not serve us well to be any less than we were intended to be. Those who hide from struggle are those that will never grow into their fullest potential. Having the courage of a hero means that you act in the face of fear and adversity. It means that you step into the arena in order to have the honor of attempting success. It is the opportunity to be in the battle that we must seek out. Never back down from the chance to demonstrate your skills as a sales warrior.

Heroic courage is not the absence of fear. It is acting in the face of fear. The third virtue of Selling With Honor is taking action and living fully into your talents, despite fear of rejection, fear of failure, or even fear of success. Too many people imagine problems and therefore freeze instead of acting. Time and time again, I have seen people who held a sales position say that they could not find success, or that nobody was buying, or that the economy was too slow to be successful. When asked how many phone calls they had made to set appointments, how many appointments they had gone on to create presentations, and how many deals they had won and how many they had lost, they stare blankly forward. If a salesperson is not in the battle, doing what is necessary to succeed, then failure is inevitable.

When I was young and in martial arts, I was initially afraid to spar. I did not want to get hurt, or even hit. It took pushing through that fear and stepping onto the mat to learn to be who I was intended to be in this life. Fear prevents us from living the life we were intended to live. Fear prevents us from picking up the phone and calling the prospect that would truly benefit from what we have to offer. Fear keeps us in our comfort zone and away from glory. One of the lessons that I learned, while studying Muay Thai, was that of winning by getting hit. I was taught to go against my natural instincts to step away from the danger of the punch or kick and step into it instead. The lesson was that the punch lacked power if I got into it before the arm was fully extended. The same thing is true about stepping into an objection. When we step away from an objection in a presentation, we lose momentum and falter. When we hit the objection head on and are willing to get knocked around a little, we significantly increase our odds of success.

If you take this principle of "stepping in" to heart, you find that you are willing to be told no repeatedly. I remember when I first began selling professional services. My objective was to be told no 30 times in 30 days. This meant that I had to be in front of quite a few people in order to be rejected that often. In martial arts, we would have a student stand in the "horse stance" and then hit them and kick them while they remained still. We didn't use a lot of force, but we did condition them to realize that they could handle any attack from any attacker. Once they had been conditioned in this manner, they would begin to step into the attack and lessen its effectiveness. The students, including myself, would learn that they did, in fact, have the capacity to stay in the arena and take the hits. In any business setting, there will be rejection. There will be times that people are not nice to you. That is simply a part of the battle.

During my 30 rejections in 30 days experiment, one of the objectives that my coach had given me was to have at least one person be angry and force me out of their office. My business coach made it into a game of sorts. Nobody pulled a gun on me or anything like that, but I did push a construction owner to take a very hard look at the way in which he and his managers were treating their employees. He was mad at me for making him recognize his faults. He yelled at me to leave his office. As I stood up, I calmly said to him, "I will be available to help you solve these challenges and get more from your people and stop losing your talent whenever you are ready." I held out my hand with my card. He did not lift his hand to take it, so I dropped it on his desk. I was never mean to him, nor did I push him in a disrespectful manner. I did, however, make him look honestly at what he already knew was wrong with his business. I did business with him a year later and helped his managers to treat their employees more respectfully. You never really know what your presentation will do for another person. Although he was angry at the time, he knew that he needed to be building a more respectful environment. If I had not been willing to take the hits, those employees never would have gotten a better place to work. I needed to know what the key was to winning the battles that I faced.

It took a full year of martial arts before I learned that courage is what unlocks the victory in the battle. Courage is what allows us to break through the board or the brick or the barrier that we are facing. It is courage that allows us to take the talents that we have and show them to the world. The warrior in sales is not without fear. He or she is simply going to act in spite of it.

We act with the courage of a hero when we have the conviction of a hero. This conviction comes from knowing that we have something that can truly make a difference in the lives of other people. In building better cultures for companies, I know beyond a shadow of a doubt that I will make a difference. My company has a very simple "why" for existence. We exist to create deeper connections, to inspire greatness, and to be an agent of positive change. We each see ourselves as agents of change and we act accordingly. When a leader identifies with the "why" of our existence, then they embrace the opportunity to work together. When they do not identify with the reason for our existence, they battle to not do business with us.

The stronger the conviction that I have and that my sales warriors have, the easier it is to inspire action from a prospect. People in this world are longing to be inspired by a hero. They are seeking ways in which to be connected with a man or woman of conviction. Heroes are so rare in this day and age that their presence is disruptive to everything around them.

Take a few moments to simply think about the positive difference that your product or service has on the clients that you serve. Visualize them receiving the service and being excited to pay for the service because you operated with honor. Try to feel the positive emotion that goes with making a difference in the life of another person. Think about the difference that you are making and how much better off that person is for knowing you. Spend a few minutes every morning seeing how your prospects will benefit from doing business with you. Imagine yourself saving the day, guiding the client to their desired future, and being a catalyst for success for your clients. When you can hold this vision in your mind, you will find that you accomplish just that. You make the lives of those around you much better.

The question that I have for you is this...

What could you accomplish if you never allowed fear to slow you down?

That question is one that continuously makes me realize that a life gripped in fear is a life of failure. Choose NOT to let fear slow you down. Admit when you are afraid and take action because of that fear. When you allow fear to grip you and control you, you never exceed a life of mediocrity.

The three main fears that seem to exist in business are...

1. The fear of failure – The fear of failure keeps people from taking action because they are afraid that they will not be successful. The interesting dilemma with the fear of failure is that without action, fear is guaranteed. People

who are afraid to fail are seldom ever successful. They remain locked into the same life day in and day out because they are not attempting the greatness that they were designed to achieve. If you find that you are suffering from the fear of failure, the best thing to do is to take a few hits. Go out and attempt to be told no at least 30 times in 30 days. Chances are you will find the same thing that I did. When I was told no 30 times, I was told yes more that month than I had ever been.

2. The fear of success – Although this sounds strange, there are countless people that are afraid of being successful. They are afraid of who they will become if they are rich, famous, and loved by everyone. They are comfortable in their life right now. They know what to expect. They are afraid of what people would want from them if they had money and power. Their fears are unfounded. The truth of the matter is that success does not change us. It amplifies us! Whoever you are now, you will simply be more of when you are successful.

3. The fear of rejection – People worry so much about what others will think of them. They worry that people, that they don't even know,

will not like them. People worry that they won't be popular in their social circle, so they freeze instead of acting. This fear is an imagined fear, just like the vast majority of them are. The funny thing is that people cannot be rejected if they don't act, but they also cannot be accepted. Countless people have not written the book in their head or taken the chance that would bring them fulfillment because of the fear of what others would think. This fear of rejection has kept people from being the hero that they were designed to be. Take the leap and see how many acceptances and how many rejections you can rack up in four weeks. You will find that even those that don't buy from you will often call you friend after you present to them.

I have seen salespeople that found it easier to put their families in poverty than to face their fears and make the calls. I have seen salespeople who found it easier to be reprimanded and even fired than it was to use their talents and implement the right behaviors to achieve success. To play the part of the hero, you must wake up every day ready to step onto the battlefield. There is no chance of victory if you are not in the battle. There is no chance of success without action.

You, and yes I mean you, can be wildly successful in sales if you will eliminate being afraid. If you will tell fear to stand aside, you astonish the world with your talent and your results. Heroic courage is what makes others stand in awe of your accomplishments. This is the virtue that keeps you moving toward all that you are capable of being! I will leave you with an excerpt from the speech "Citizenship In A Republic" by Theodore Roosevelt.

It is not the critic who counts; not the man who points out how the strong man stumbles, or where the doer of deeds could have done them better. The credit belongs to the man who is actually in the arena, whose face is marred by dust and sweat and blood; who strives valiantly; who errs, who comes short again and again, because there is no effort without error and shortcoming; but who does actually strive to do the deeds; who knows great enthusiasms, the great devotions; who spends himself in a worthy cause; who at the best knows in the end the triumph of high achievement, and who at the worst, if he fails, at least fails while daring greatly, so that his place shall never be with those cold and timid souls who neither know victory nor defeat.

Never find yourself in the position of stepping off of the battlefield. Never be one of the people who knows neither victory nor defeat. To be a hero, you must act as a hero would act. You must be willing to take action at every turn and do, every day, the actions that keep you in the battle. You are a hero. You act in the face of fear. You achieve success because you never give up.

Your mantra as a hero:

I am a hero. I bring honor to my profession and success to my clients. I am a hero. I wake up every day knowing that I have a higher purpose and knowing that I must take action to ensure that others have the chance to succeed as a result of what I offer. I am a hero. I take action every day and will achieve victory because I will never give up. I am a hero.

What will you do in order to live the life of a hero today and every day?

_____

_____

_____

_____

_____

CHAPTER 4
THE 4TH VIRTUE – HONOR

Meiyo, or honor, is the fourth virtue of Bushido Sales. You cannot hide from yourself. In that still dark place, the one in which only you can exist, the truth is still with you. The truth still illuminates who you are. You are a reflection of the behaviors that you exhibit and the choices that you make. To be honorable in selling, you must display honor in all of your decisions. You can only bring honor to your employer if you evaluate every choice that you make from the perspective of what the honorable thing would be to do.

THE CHOICES

The sales warrior knows that their honor is a direct reflection of how they make decisions and defines who they truly are as a person. There are three questions that will help you to make honorable choices in selling and in presenting what you have to offer.

1. Is this what is best for the client or customer? When evaluating what is best for the client or customer, you have to weigh the options. You have to look at the price of the solution versus what they are spending right now. You have to look at the strategic direction of the company and ensure that you are supporting their desired direction. You also have to ensure that the solution you are offering will leave them better than you found them.

2. Will this meet the needs and/or desires of the customer? In your sales interview, you should uncover what direction the customer/client wants to go. By understanding what is important to them, you become a part of their team. Think of yourself as an extension of their leadership team with the same strategic objectives as they have. Your job is to find the best possible deal for the client that meets their needs and wants, and that solves the challenge that they are facing.

3. Will this be profitable for my employer? If

you are your own employer, the question still remains. You have to find a solution that is good for both the customer and your employer. You cannot give away your services or your products. You must find the win-win solution that leaves both parties satisfied and feeling better for having been a part of the process. You have to make money. The employer has to make money. The customer has to benefit through cost reduction, increased profit, or some other measurement of success.

By willingly addressing these questions up-front, you will find that you keep your focus more on producing measurable results. It is the measurement of success that is the validation of success in any endeavor.

UNDERSTANDING YOU

In studying martial arts, the premise of learning to fight in the Eastern arts has always been to understand and then shape who you really are. Honor, to the warrior, is more valuable than any material possession. It is all that they are and all that they can be. Your honor is your reputation. It is the sum total of the choices that you have made and the actions that you have taken. Here is a short exercise to help you establish the reputation that you want.

List the 3 values that are most important to you.

These are the values that you would never give up for any reason. They are critically important to you. Name the value and explain why it is important to you.

MY VALUES

1. _____

_____

_____

2. _____

_____

_____

3. _____

_____

_____

Make sure that you name the value and explain why it is important to you or how you came to see the importance of it.

SOCIAL STANDING

In the Bushido, your social standing, your very worth as a person, was based on your honor. Your honor was measured by the harmonic relationship between your actions and the code of conduct outlined in the Bushido. Sales is no different today. In order to live with honor, one must operate within the code of conduct outlined by the company and with absolute integrity. You will want to take it one step further, though. You will want to outline your own code of conduct that you will live by. An example of a code that you could live by is…

- I will give all that I have, each day, to my profession. I will stay focused and do all of the necessary actions of a successful sales warrior each and every day that I work.

- I will always strive to find solutions that are beneficial to my clients and profitable to my employer.

- I will tell the truth in all things. I will not make excuses for any action or any shortcoming. I will examine myself and find the truth.

- I will honor my family by providing for them. I will work diligently to be the highest version of myself and to provide a life that they are proud of and that honors them.

- I will honor myself by doing all that I am capable of doing. I will astonish myself with the effort that I give and the results that I achieve.

- I will keep myself balanced. I will spend time keeping myself in shape mentally through study, physically through exercise, and spiritually through connection.

- I will honor my coworkers by supporting and encouraging them. I will be positive and will help them to focus on the good that exists in our jobs, our company, our community, and our world.

- I will honor my neighbors by being positive and by helping when I am able.

- I will honor those in need by putting myself in a position that I am able to give and give freely. I will be successful so that I might help others raise their position in life.

- I will live an honorable life by evaluating all that I do and ensuring that it is the right thing before I do it as well as after it is done.

CHOOSE WHO YOU WILL HONOR

The question that many will ask is, "Who do I honor?" This question is answered in 3 parts.

1. You honor yourself. By honoring yourself, you are living a life and facilitating the solution of people's problems in such a way that you, or anyone observing, would see that you had the customer's best interests at heart. You honor yourself when you know that you can lay your head down at night and know that you have done your best and provided the best you could.

2. You honor your company. By honoring your company, you are giving your best effort, your best communication, your utmost integrity, and your absolute focus to accomplish the vision of the organization. The Samurai would honor and obey the emperor even if they disagreed with the direction they were taking the country because that is what was right. Too often, people want to be insubordinate to their boss, or rude to their customer, or sabotage their company. This is living a life without honor. The honorable life strives to bring success to all that it serves.

3. You honor your customer. You do not live your life for the sale. Instead, you live your life to provide solutions for others. You listen to your customer, truly listen. You collaborate with them to find the right solutions, even if that sometimes means that it is not with you. You honor your customer by living a life of integrity.

THE PAST, PRESENT, AND FUTURE

People often long for the good 'ol days, when things were the way they were supposed to be. They think back to when they were young, the music was good, and people could be trusted to do what they said they were going to do for the price they said they were going to do it. They look back as if there is no hope of that world existing in the present or in the future. What happened in the past was simply a series of choices. Anyone can make a choice. Everyone does make a choice. It is up to you to make the choice each day when you rise to live your life so that others will be proud of the results that you achieve.

Gandhi was one of the leaders that has always fascinated me. He was an incredible salesperson, yet most people don't think of him that way. He persuaded a country to be peaceful and another country to leave. He persuaded the British empire to peacefully choose to leave India. He sold them on the benefits of going in a different direction after hundreds of years. Consider this… the most honorable salesperson will always give the customer or client a choice. In Gandhi's case, Britain fully believed that it made the choice to leave. They believed it was what was best for them and what was best for India. Gandhi chose to live with honor in that moment. As a result, he changed the course of the future. The greatest sales warriors understand that they can choose the values that they admire from the past and live into those values in the present. As a result, they continuously shape the future!

One's reputation is ultimately all that they have in this world. Sales warriors value that reputation above all else. They know that it is their service that sets them apart from others. They live by the principle of always providing more service and better service than they were paid to provide. They never sacrifice long-term honor for short-term gain. They measure their choices and are deliberate about their actions. They give all that they have, every day. They are never lazy. They never take advantage of their employer. They are grateful for their opportunity and make the most of it through action and positive results.

Honor yourself. Honor your boss. Honor your company. Live the sales warrior's life in such a way that you sleep peacefully at night, work diligently during the day, and are respected by those around you!

The following is how I will show honor to my employer, my clients, and myself.

_____

_____

_____

_____

CHAPTER 5
THE 5TH VIRTUE – COMPASSION

The sales warrior is disciplined and skilled. They possess the power to persuade and move people to action. Because their power is strong, they remain tempered with compassion for their fellow man. The term compassion originally meant "to feel with." This indicates a connectedness that is truly beneficial to both the customer and the salesperson. When a sales warrior is connected with the person that they are helping, then they are seeking what would be good for that person. It is the desire to do what is right for another person that keeps the sales warrior on the right path. Without this connection, it would be impossible to live by the code.

As a 9 year-old in martial arts, I was in there for the same reason as most other young men. I wanted to become centered. Just kidding. I was in there because I wanted to learn to "kick butt." It was the desire for power and dominance over others that attracted me to the sport originally. I wanted to be able to reposition myself in life.

I thought that there would be an incredible power with not being the short kid that got picked on. But what I found was so much more. I found that the real power was in not using my art in a negative way. The real power was in being able to help others who could not help themselves. Sales really flows along that same path. When you, as a sales warrior, go into a presentation, it should not be about your incredible power to persuade people to buy what you are selling. Instead, it should be about connecting with that prospect in an attempt to fully understand what they are looking for and what they need. When you can garner that deeper understanding, you will be in a position to meet their needs and their wants. You will not be persuading or coercing them into anything at that point. Instead, you will be facilitating them getting what they wanted anyway. A big part of your role is to keep people from buying things that will not move them forward. You are there as their personal defender.

I remember defending several people in my life who

did not feel that they could stand up for themselves. I remember taking the successes that I had in life financially and helping others who needed a hand up or a boost. I have done these things because they were the right thing to do. I have also been compassionate towards prospects in pointing out that it was not me that they needed, or my products. There are times that showing compassion is simply pointing people in the right direction, even when they are wanting to give you money. It is more important to solve their challenges than it is to sell your training, or your software, or your technology.

If you do have the answer to their challenge, the only compassionate thing that you can do is to allow them to buy from you so that their challenge is solved and the problem no longer exists. If you do NOT have the answer to their challenge, then the only compassionate choice that exists is to help them find a better solution provider. You have a product or service that provides value. It provides more value than it costs, which is why people want to purchase from you.

Helping others does not mean giving your stuff away. I want to caution you that if people don't have any level of commitment, then they will also not take the solution as serious. Your goal has to be the true betterment of the person or the client. That means that they must work for the solution as well. If they are not putting in effort, then you are not helping.

One of the most effective ways to ensure that you are being compassionate is to follow the use of a sales interview instead of a sales presentation. The presentation indicates that you have a preconceived notion of what the prospect should buy. The sales interview is a discovery process that unlocks what they are looking for instead of implanting what they should look for. The following is an example from my company.

In this grouping of areas, which three are the most important to you?

Feedback	Increasing Sales	Retention of Top Performers
Selection of Employees	Talent Development	Engagement
Performance Management	Other?	

Of the three that you chose, which one would you want our company to have the greatest impact on in the next 60 days? In other words, if I had a magic wand and could make anything better quickly, which one would it be?

What are you currently doing in that area?

What does your current solution not provide for you that you really wished that it would? What's missing?

Would you be interested in exploring how my organization could fill that gap and help you achieve your goals for a reasonable price?

This simple interview is a way to get the prospect to identify what is important to them. We must understand what is important and what they feel is missing in order to compassionately fill that need. Think about your organization and what the primary areas of service are that you offer. Could you come up with a similar question set that would lead people down the right path and solve their challenges? Any organization can be compassionate by first deciding to listen more than they talk. They must be willing to ask questions instead of simply telling the customer what they want to sell to them.

There are a number of organizations that seem to forget that the objective must always be to meet the needs of the customer instead of the needs of the salesperson. When an advertising organization, such as a newspaper has not sold all of their ad space, the sales manager will often tell the sales reps to get out there and fill the paper. So, the reps get on the phone and "push their product." I relate this to the "drug dealer" model. It isn't about what is best for the customer or even what will actually work for them. It is only about deadlines and profits. If an advertising rep cares about their customer, then they are seeking to understand the needs, wants, and motives of the customer. By doing this, they are positioning themselves to be the customer's greatest advocate. When we interview our customers and listen to their needs, we focus on what is good for them over what is profitable to us.

At every turn in your sales journey, seek out ways to help others, to make their lives richer and more successful. Show your compassion for the client by providing the best solution that you can provide and working towards solving their problems. If you do this, the reward will follow. You will not have to worry about the money, only the solution. It is an interesting paradox that when we serve our customer, they seek out ways to honor us with their business. When we take advantage of our customer, they seek out ways to avoid us. It is your reputation that will precede you. Are you getting results or simply selling products?

The compassionate sales warrior always puts the needs of their customer ahead of their own profits!

CHAPTER 6
THE 6TH VIRTUE – SINCERITY

6th Virtue of Bushido Sales

The 6th Virtue of Bushido Sales is Makato, or
sincerity. Sincerity is the harmony between thoughts,
words, and actions. It is when we know in our hearts
that we are being the best version of ourselves. When
your thoughts are in alignment with your words and
your words are in alignment with your actions, you
can be trusted. You have a presence about you. Some
people will call it your aura, others your energy field,
some relate it to your communication micro-
expressions. Whichever way you choose to look at it,
your inner thought world is portrayed in your outer
world.

There are too many people in this world that are trying to fool others. They are trying to convince them to buy things that even the salesperson doesn't believe in. You are not that person. You know that the greatest salespeople in the world, the ones that appear to be sales warriors, spend time fully understanding what amazing things their product or service can do. They study it and find ways that it can reshape the lives of others. They do not make things up about their product or service. They are open, honest, and direct about what they are able to do in helping their clients. They believe in their product and they believe in themselves. They know that they will produce results.

The sales warrior can be counted on to follow through on anything they indicate will be done. They are always true to their word. There is no need for them to promise because their indication of commitment is a promise in and of itself. Think back two or three generations. Close your eyes and imagine what it meant for a person to shake another person's hand and commit to a course of action. When a man or woman gave their word, it was their bond. Now close your mind's eye and imagine going back four hundred years to the days of the Samurai. Block out everything else around you and focus just on the following thoughts.

Imagine that your world was based on reputation.

Your very worth was based on you doing what you said that you would do. Feel the emotions that are connected with being sincere. Feel the positive feeling of telling a person that you will deliver results, that you will protect them, and then feel how incredible it feels to actually deliver. Now imagine yourself as a different person, still in the days of old. Imagine that you have indicated that you will protect a person and they believed in you. Imagine that you simply did not do your job and they were hurt. You know and they know that you were able to protect them. You simply did not choose to do what would have been honorable. You become unsure of whether you can trust yourself and they are sure that you cannot be trusted. Notice how different it feels to live with the honor of truth versus the dishonor. A sales warrior always lives and dies with honor.

Too many times in this world, sales people will say anything to get the deal. It is a little scary how many people know going into a buying decision that they cannot trust the word of the salesperson. They know that much of what has been indicated will never happen. Sales should be a very honorable profession. There are organizations that bring shame to it and individuals that dishonor it through their beliefs, thoughts, actions, and deception, though. Think about the used car business. Think about what image pops into your head when I refer to a used car salesperson. Is it a positive image or a negative image?

What image pops into your head when I refer to an insurance salesperson? When enough people in a given industry operate without sincerity, the reputation of the entire industry is damaged.

How much do you believe of what comes out of the mouth of an insurance salesperson? How much do you believe of what comes out of the mouth of a used car salesperson? If you, as a buyer, are going into the sales situation without being confident that the salesperson has your best interest at heart, how does your attitude change? Many people have had these negative experiences with those industries. There are certainly other industries that have posed problems as well, but let's focus on these two for now. What do you do when you find a used car salesperson or an insurance salesperson that is completely honest with you, that you feel is sincere? Do you tell others? Do you brag about doing business with them?

From my own experience, when I found a car salesperson that was honest and sincere, I began talking about that person in speeches and writing about them in blogs. I sent more than 2 dozen people to buy cars from this person in 24 months, and they all bought. Because this person was honest and sincere with me, I entrusted my friends to them. I brought them 1 new sale per month for over 2 years. When salespeople think that they will do better by being dishonest, they are very short-sighted. They cannot see the future or choose not to think about the long-term. They chase short-term money, which is always, always, always less in the long-run. Within one year of beginning a sales career, you will have a reputation as either a person that can be trusted or a person that cannot be trusted. The choice is yours. Will you choose to live a sincere life?

The true salesperson does not live by a false code. They live a life that is pure and honorable. In Og Mandino's book, <u>The Greatest Salesman In The World,</u> he tells of how the Apostle Paul sold the Gospel of Jesus Christ. He tells of ancient scrolls that mapped out the patterns of success necessary for becoming the greatest salesman in the world. One virtue that is consistent in all books teaching long-term successful relationships with clients is that of being sincere. Whether you are reading Og Mandino, Zig Ziglar, Napoleon Hill, or other great authors, you will find that sincerity is central to true success.

If you were to look at the interactions that you have with clients, can you say that you follow through on what you say you will do? Or, do you struggle with being on top of things? Are you completely honest about what you are able to do to help a client succeed or do you embellish the truth with what you think the client wants to hear or needs to hear to buy from you?

Write out your personal statement about being a

sincere person on the next page. An example would be: I will choose, each day, to live a sincere life. I will be honest in all of my dealings. I will do what I say I will do and I will deliver positive results. Okay, now it is your turn.

_____

_____

_____

_____

_____

_____

_____

Being a sales warrior requires you to be genuine and sincere. Live and sell in a such a way that you would be honored to buy from yourself. Live by this code and watch your sales flourish!

CHAPTER 7
THE 7TH VIRTUE – LOYALTY

Chu, or Loyalty, is the 7th Virtue of Bushido
Sales. The sales warrior is fiercely responsible for
their actions, their words and for the care of those
whom they work for and with. This would include
their employer, their coworkers, and their clients.
They have a sense of pride in taking care of the needs
of others and strive to honor them by doing their very
best. To be loyal is to be honest, of good heart,
trustworthy, and consistently focused on delivering
the promised results. At times, loyalty can be difficult
to spot. Disloyalty, however, is always easy to spot. It
is marked by deception and self-absorption. The loyal
salesperson is a proud and integral part of the

company for which they work.

They never look for an excuse or a way to avoid their duties. They take pleasure and pride in performing the duties of their job each and every day. They understand that serving with joy is a choice and make that choice each day as they arise. They accept the responsibility that is theirs for the choices they make and the actions they take. Think about how different life would be if you never made an excuse for any result or action. What if you viewed every one of your actions as a choice that you made? How different would your life be at that point? How different would life be if the people around you stopped making excuses and accepted responsibility for their actions? It would be shocking, and significantly more would be accomplished.

When a sales warrior enters into a contract with an employer, they willingly and purposefully give all of who they are to ensure the success of the venture. They don't make excuses. They achieve results. Even the mediocre salesperson has the capacity for success if they devote themselves to that endeavor. Even the best salesperson has the possibility of failure when they choose NOT to perform the necessary actions of success. To give one's all to an employer means that they are focused on the employer and the success of the organization with every fiber of their being during work hours. Most likely, they will even be thinking

about ways to make the employer more successful
when they are outside of working hours. What have
you done to demonstrate loyalty to your employer? If
you are your employer, the question remains the
same. Take a minute to answer that in the blanks
below.

_____

_____

_____

_____

_____

The sales warrior feels an intense obligation to the
product or service that they are evangelizing and
believe wholeheartedly in their pursuit. They would
never dishonor themselves by selling something that
they would not use or could not support. There are
far too many people in this world that are working
without purpose. You must understand "WHY" your
product or service exists. You must understand
"WHY" your company exists. It is the "WHY" that
ultimately matters the most. Simon Sinek, in his
YouTube video titled, "Golden Circles," talks about
what great companies know that others do not. The
greatest companies in the world begin with why
instead of what. The mediocre and the failing

companies begin with what they do, then how they do it, and never address why they are doing what they do. Companies that change the landscape of reality are those that have an intense understanding of why they are doing what they do, and then they outline how they will do it. At this point, the customer identifies with the values of the organization and/or the salesperson so intensely that they would buy almost any "what" that existed for the company. Take a few minutes to answer two questions.

1. Why is this product or service important and why does it exist?

_____

_____

_____

_____

_____

2. Why are you a part of this organization and why is your job important?

_____

_____

_____

_____

_____

Once a true loyalty exists, there is very little that could ever stand in the way of the sales warrior. They are loyal because that is what they are made to do. They are loyal because it is an integral part of their definition of self. Their loyalty is not dependent on outside circumstances. It is a choice that they gladly make every day. Their loyalty inspires commitment in themselves as well as in those with whom they have contact. Coworkers, employees, vendors, and clients are all inspired to return the loyalty that they have experienced. It is a rare event to be inspired and people embrace it when the opportunity arises.

Upon the commitment to the duty, the sales warrior sees only the end result and will move heaven and earth to attain that end result. The sales warrior does not behave as an employee that wishes to be cared for. Instead, they feel a sense of duty to ensure that others have a job and an ever-increasing opportunity. They see themselves as the catalyst for success for those they work with and take pride in bringing opportunities to their fellow employees. What are three things that you could begin doing today that would create more security and opportunity for the company and for the others that work at your organization?

_____

_____

_____

_____

_____

_____

_____

_____

_____

_____

They develop and hone their skills because their loyalty brings with it a sense of duty and honor. Their duty is derived from the continued development of their character, the core of who they are. This character exists at all times and is not turned on or off at certain times of the day. They know that character is who they are and who they are is not varied based on their job. They consistently choose to perform better than they have done in the past. They strive for continuous and never-ending improvement. They behave the way that they do because it is a reflection of who they are at their core. It is how they see themselves in every minute of every day.

It is who they are and how they behave in every situation of life. This means that whether they are at work, in a social setting, or at home, they strive to bring honor to themselves and those around them. Their behaviors are their moral expectation of themselves. To do any less than their best would be to dishonor themselves. They would not choose to do any less than all they are capable of doing because that would go against their vision of themselves.

Loss of honor is the greatest failure of the sales warrior and directly violates the Sales Bushido. In the next chapter on Selling With Honor, the sales warrior demonstrates what must be done if they have chosen the path of failure.

Success or failure is but a choice to be made.

CHAPTER 8
SEPPUKKU

Seppukku – Honor is our guide

I would like to start this section by stating that it is not my intention to get people to quit their jobs. It is my observation that a large number (76% according to Career Builder) of people are unhappy in their jobs. In sales, as many as 80% of people could be considered unsuccessful. This is primarily from people entering the sales arena without the full intent of success. They thought that salespeople made great money, but did not study the craft of selling. Those who choose not to perform the behaviors of successful people would honor their employer by stepping out of the way so that someone who is willing to perform those duties may step in and bring success to their employer. The rest of this book describes the final virtue of the bushido sales warrior.

Seppuku was a ritual suicide that a Samurai would perform if they had been defeated in battle or had dishonored the code. Although extreme to us, it was a sign of true honor to know when you had been defeated as a warrior and to release your spirit from its defeated body. In Bushido Sales, the sales warrior puts forth all of their effort, their complete focus on success. There are times, however, when they are not selling the right product or service, or when they are not right for sales. If they have done all that they could and behaved as a sales warrior would behave, yet they have still been defeated on the field of honor, they will end their career with that company. If they have been unwilling to perform the behaviors of a successful sales warrior, they are bound by honor to step out of the way by ending their career with that company.

They will not linger around the company because it is safe to stay there. They will not continue to take money from the company that they cannot bring honor to. They will humbly and gratefully walk away. They will thank their employer for the opportunity that had been set before them, but will realize when it is time to move on. This is not an easy decision for the Bushido Sales Warrior, for they will have devoted their time and their talent and their emotions into bringing success to their art. This will be a deep decision that brings honor to themselves and to their employer. They will make way for others to find success in that role and will honor their employer in thought, word, and deed.

In this case, Seppuku is not the ending of a life, but the ending of a career that was not bringing success to themselves or their employer. The sales warrior knows that success in their endeavors is the true path and if that path cannot be attained, they willingly make way for someone who can fulfill the path. This would happen for a very small percentage of sales warriors, because the Bushido Sales Warrior would have put in all of the necessary effort to succeed before this conclusion could be reached. Do all that you can to succeed for all the right reasons, with the right people and the right product/service.

Always Be Honest With Yourself and Honor Those That Provide You With Opportunity.

CHAPTER 9
CONSULTATIVE SELLING

Consultative selling is one of the easiest ways to live and sell with honor. The process can be broken down into 3 steps. If you will follow these 3 steps, you will not only be an honorable salesperson, you will be a very successful one. The precursor to this has been discussed throughout this book. You must be disciplined and willing to put forth the effort to be successful. Assuming that you are a driven and focused person, the rest is simply flow.

STEP 1 – TRUST
It takes trust for a person to have faith. In order for a client to have faith in you and your product/service, they must trust you. This is not

about the reputation of the company nearly as much as it is about the interaction that you are having with them. I am going to assume that you would only work for an honorable company. Therefore, the reputation of the company is presumably solid and honorable. In order for the person to trust you, you will have to choose which path it will take to establish their trust and faith in you.

Proof before payment, sometimes known as the "freemium" model is one way to get there. This is where you have something of value to offer to your prospects. This allows them to engage with you without risking any money. They have the chance to see the way that you will work and to try out your product/service. This is a great way to operate, particularly in a world where people are continuously chasing the "quick buck." Deliver results just as you would if they were paying for the service. By doing this, you are being sincere in how you would conduct yourself and they are seeing the real you and the real version of the company that you represent.

Guaranteed results is another way that you can go. This path will require that you have absolute faith in yourself and know, without any doubt, that you can and will deliver results. I used this model quite a bit in the beginning of my business. I knew in my heart that I could and would deliver results. I was so confident in that result that I staked not just my reputation, but 100% of the cost, including travel, on the fact that I could deliver. I helped to increase leadership capacity and reduced turnover. I would guarantee a 50% reduction in turnover from wherever the company was at that point, if they participated from the top down in my full program. I was willing to return all monies for an entire year if I did not deliver. This earned me a great reputation and it demonstrated that I fully believed what I was saying.

The next methodology to create trust is to connect through activities outside of work. When you connect with people through giving a sincere effort in volunteer settings and giving fully of your talents, you will find that people connect deeply with you. Whether you are volunteering for a leadership organization or helping at your local soup kitchen, give all of who you are to the volunteer effort. Get involved in something that you believe in. Don't do this just to connect with people. Do this because it represents your beliefs and it is a part of who you are. You should never be disingenuous. Instead, be the best version of yourself and throw yourself into making a difference in the activities that you get involved with. This will help to build trust and it will make a positive impact at the same time.

STEP 2 – DISCOVERY

Once you have established trust with your prospect, you will be able to uncover what they are needing and wanting. One thing that is critical to remember is that people buy what they believe they need and want. They don't buy what you want to sell. Make your interactions wholly about what they need, what they want, and where they would like to see themselves go in the future. The process that is recommended is to outline 10 or fewer areas that impact the success of their organization or their personal success in a graphic format. Use this graphic to slide in front of them and ask them the following...

Of the areas listed on this sheet, which three are the most important to you and your organization?

Give them the opportunity to study the sheet and to choose the three that are most important to them. After they have indicated which three are critical, you will ask them to whittle it down a little more. The second question that you ask is...

Of those three areas, which one would be the most critical for us to have a positive impact on in the next 60 to 90 days?

This is generally a pretty easy answer for the customer. Pay attention and write down the one that is most critical. After they tell you which one is the most important, you will ask the next question...

Why is that one the most important?

This will get them thinking about their current situation and will help them to remember the pain that exists with that area not going the way that it should and the pleasure associated with it going perfectly. They may pause a little in their answer, but they will almost always have an answer. Next, you will ask...

What are doing currently to ensure that you achieve your desired results in that area?

Many times, they are not doing anything to solve the challenge that they are facing in the area that they have indicated is most important to them. This will really solidify in their mind that they are frustrated with where they are and that they really do desire to move themselves and/or their business forward. If they do have something that they are doing, which may be something just to make themselves not look like they are doing nothing, you will still want to take notes and listen intently. After you have listened to what they had to say, you will ask the follow up question to that question, which is…

What do you wish you had in the way of results, that you don't currently have from the solution or direction that is in place?

By asking this, you are getting them to open up and explain the "gap" that exists between their present reality and their desired reality. People always buy "the gap." Very seldom, do they buy a product or service. They are buying a solution that will move them from where they are to where they want to be. If your product or service can move them from their existing situation to the place they want to be, then you will very likely have a new client or customer. The trial closing question that seems to work very well is…

If I can come up with a way to get you where you want to go for a reasonable price, would you be interested?

You are discovering if they really want to solve the problem or not. If they say yes, you will want to prepare a proposal that outlines where they are, where they want to be, and how you will help them get there. If they say that they would not be interested, ask the following...

Help me understand why you would not want to solve the problem that is important to you.

This will make them talk about why they don't want to move forward and will help you to determine whether or not you wish to continue the conversation with them. If they truly don't want to move forward, it is best to let them know that you will be there for them when they are ready, but not to push them too hard. Selling with honor and being a sales warrior will require you to know when to step away and when to advance.

STEP 3 – PROOF

As the Jell-O commercials in the 1980's used to say, "The proof is in the pudding." Once a person is using your product or service, are they actually getting what you had promised them? If they are getting the results that you indicated, then you are an honorable sales warrior. If they are not getting what you promised, then you need to go out of your way to ensure that those right results are achieved. Keeping your promises is critical to your long-term success and it is a reflection of who you are at your core. If you regularly promise things that you cannot or will not deliver, then you are not living with honor. You should always render more service and better service than the customer or client expects from you. If you will make it your habit to go beyond what you are paid to do with every client, then you will never hurt for clients. You will have an abundance of people who desire to work with you.

PEOPLE WILL ALWAYS BUY YOU BEFORE THEY BUY YOUR PRODUCT OR SERVICE.

CHAPTER 10 - BONUS SECTION
THE 7 STEPS OF SELLING

There are 7 steps in the selling process. Once a person masters these 7 steps, they will see significant increases in their ability to build business and assist their clients in achieving their goals. The 7 steps are...

Networking - This is the process of building your positive reputation and creating mutually beneficial relationships.

Prospecting - This is the process of identifying people that your product or service will assist.

Discovery - This is the process of setting appointments and interviewing prospects to discover what fit, if any, exists for your product or service within their organization.

The Move - This is the component of presenting back to the prospect what they are wanting to accomplish and how your product or service will help them get there. The intent is to move them from prospect to client through a signatory commitment to their enhanced future success or happiness through what you provide.

The Delivery - This is the component of the sale where you provide the product or service that the new client/customer has purchased. Never underestimate the importance of the relationship at this point. How you deliver your product or service will determine whether or not you are able to complete the next step in the process.

The Re-Buy - This is the portion of the interaction where the customer/client purchases more of your product or service, or they expand the spectrum of purchases.

The Referral - This is the portion of the interaction where the customer/client tells their friends, relatives, and associates about what you have to offer and how it has made their life better.

NETWORKING

Networking - This is the process of building your positive reputation and creating mutually beneficial relationships.

Networking in order to build your business is all about creating meaningful connections and having something to offer. The component that I see missed more often than anything else is the "having something to offer" piece. Most people will simply try to shove their stuff on others. This is not an offering! It is pushy and annoying. As you build your network, you want to focus on associating with people that exist in the realm that you need to be in. In my book, <u>Leadership Evo</u>, I talk about the power of association. Who you associate with is who you become like. In business networking, you want to associate with successful people and those who are willing to push themselves, sacrifice, and drive hard for success. These are the individuals that will end up wanting what you have to offer. They will want it because they will relate to you and admire something in who you are.

What you have to offer is yourself. Never go into any relationship looking for what you can get. Instead, go into relationships looking for what you can give. If your objective is to help others reach their goals and attain their success, then your success is inevitable. If your objective is to sell stuff to other people, you may close some deals, but you will also close a lot of doors. Keep in mind that people enjoy buying stuff. They simply don't enjoy being sold stuff. That is why you take the "other-centered" approach in the networking process.

The three steps that you must follow to be a successful networker are...

1. Listen - In any relationship, whether on-line or in-person, your first priority should be to listen for how the person has related to what you offer, what they think about it and what they would like to see that they don't currently have. If you focus on asking questions and listening actively to the other person, they will tell you whether or not they are a good potential prospect. If they are not, don't push them that way. If they are, the process will flow naturally because you listened the way you were supposed to listen.

2. Engage - Your second objective should be to engage the person in the relationship so that they desire to be around you. It is through meaningful conversation and adaptive communication that you move the person into engagement. Engaged people focus on connecting with you. Disengaged people focus on getting away from you. We waste too much time trying to convince others that we are awesome and not enough time convincing them that they are the awesome ones and will

be even more-so when we are working together.

3. Give - The third objective should be to give something of value to the person. This could be book recommendations, tid-bits of useful information, or guidance as they are trying to solve a problem. You will not move people into real prospects if you don't have anything to offer them or if you focus on taking from them. Be a giver, not a taker!

In all of your conversations, whether virtual or live, you must focus on getting a "L.E.G." up on your competition by being the right person yourself. When you are the person that others will benefit from being around, you will quickly and easily move people into the prospecting stage. If you are simply a "product pusher," you will agitate people. Some will buy from you to get rid of you, but none will truly respect you for your art and your craft. Networking is absolutely essential to your success. Your networking becomes the essence of who you are as a person.

PROSPECTING

Prospecting – This is the process of identifying people that your product or service will assist.

Prospecting isn't really an art. It is more of a science. I say it is a science because there is a systematic way to create predictable results. In three easy steps you can begin focusing on the right people for you and the right product/service for the people who need it.

1. Define exactly what you have to offer and how you can help others. You have to know your product/service extremely well. By knowing what problem or challenge your product/service solves, you will be able to articulate your value proposition. There are countless sales people floating around this world without a clear definition of how they can help. They come up with catchy elevator pitches and fancy ways of "pushing" what they have to offer, but that is not what people want from the sales rep.
2. Define the ideal customer that you want to serve. This second piece to the prospecting puzzle is equally as challenging for most sales reps. I hear them say things like, "what I have

is for everybody." That isn't true! We spend an inordinate amount of time trying to convince people to do business with us. If we have defined our ideal customer, we will keep our focus on those who can, will, and want to buy from us. If you think your market is "everyone," you will experience the frustration of repetitive rejection. After all, people don't like to be sold. They like to buy.

3. Identify the place that your ideal customers are and find a way to add value. By figuring out what your ideal customer profile is, you will be able to outline where they go and what they are involved in. Next, you find a way to contribute in that area. Don't go in there to sell. Go in there to offer value. When your focus is on giving, particularly during the prospecting stage, you create a pull towards you. It is that pull that is needed to get your potential prospects to become actual prospects. When they are ready for help, you simply have to be there and be ready.

Being ready to offer value allows you to propel the prospect into the next step in the sales process.

DISCOVERY

Discovery - This is the process of setting appointments and interviewing prospects to discover what fit, if any, exists for your product or service within their organization.

One of the toughest lessons that I have learned in my career in selling is when to walk away. Most of us believe that our product, service, non-profit mission, etc. is perfect for everyone. People tell me regularly that everyone needs what they have. You ask who their target customer is, and they respond with... anyone that is breathing. I have seen this to be especially true in the MLM world. The hard truth is that there are people that are not ideal for us to do business with. The key is to quickly identify if you are a fit for where that business or person wants to go. If you focus on that, you are actually honoring the other person and what is important to them. This can be done easily through a series of strategic questions and good listening. You can fail miserably in sales, especially "concept sales," if you don't follow this pattern.

Ultimately, your choice to succeed or fail is yours. It will be based on your willingness to learn and master the skills of selling. It is NOT based on the market,

the economy, your location, or any outside factor. It
is based on you!

When you are calling an organization, it is important
to know who you want to talk to before you
call. This isn't always possible. Sometimes, the
information is hidden. If you can ask for a person by
their first name, it makes getting to that person much
easier. For example, if I am wanting to talk with
Steven Smith from the ABC company, I would call
and say the following. "Hi, this is Jody. Is Steven
available?... Steven Smith." I want to come across as
personable as possible. The confidence that you have
in your tone is very important. It is also very
important to come across as if you and Steven are
buddies. This makes a huge difference in the mind of
the receptionist. Being confident, warm and friendly
with the receptionist is a requirement for this to
work. Once you are on the phone with Steven, the
conversation should go something like this...

This is Steven.
Steven, this is Jody Holland with Jody Holland
Training & Speaking. I wanted to ask for 3 1/2
minutes of your time. I only have 3 questions that I
would like to ask you to see if there is any fit for me
to help you achieve your people objectives. May I
have permission to ask you those 3 questions?

Um, if you can do that in 3 1/2 minutes, sure.

Great! First, have you ever hired or inherited
someone that you ended up wishing you had not
met? (Make a note of yes or no.)

Next, would you be interested in have the secret strategies that top companies use to increase employee engagement, reduce turnover, and make higher profits? (Make a note of yes or no.)

Finally, would it make a positive impact if your people desired to give you an average of 30% greater effort? (Make a note of yes or no.) If Steven answered yes, then you indicate that you would like to set up a time to ask him a few more key questions to discover ways that you can help him achieve his objectives. If the answer is no, you thank him for his time and ask if you can send him a short email, no mailing list stuff, with information about your company just in case he knows someone who does have the frustration of wanting to achieve the things you discussed but not having the tools. If he says no, leave him alone. If he says yes, you get his email and you have an email ready to go right then.

The key here is to ask questions, not pitch products. If you are pitching, you are annoying. If you are asking, they are buying.

THE MOVE

The Move - This is the component of presenting back to the prospect what they are wanting to accomplish and how your product or service will help them get there. The intent is to move them from prospect to client through a signatory commitment to their enhanced future success or happiness through what you provide.

This may sound a little grandiose for someone who is not trying to meet the actual needs of a client. To those whose intent is to discover the needs and then fulfill the needs of the client, this is right on target. In order to move someone into action, your objective is really to unlock what they are looking for and help them get there. You will follow a few basic steps in the conversation that will lead to the prospect becoming a valued client.

1. You must be an active listener. This means that you are engaged in the process of helping the prospect identify what they have, what they want, and what is missing. Your job is never to tell them what they need! Your job is to listen to what their needs are and make every effort to assist them in meeting those needs. You can only be noble in moving the

client into action if you have uncovered their needs and wants.

2. You must provide a great review of what they want and need. This means that you must have an accurate synopsis of what they indicated that they would like to have that they don't currently have. As you are feeding back what you heard them say, it is perfectly okay to clarify why those things are important by asking good questions.

3. Finally, you must ask if this is something that they actually want to be better. This may sound a little strange, considering they just said it was something they wanted, but you need to verify. There are people that like to talk about what needs to change, but they don't like to actually make things better.

After you listen, review, and verify, you are ready to ask for the business. It should go something like this.

You indicated that building the leadership skills of your team is very important. According to what you said, you don't have anything in place right now to make that happen, but you want something to be implemented within the next 2 months. You indicated that you know that things won't get better by doing the same thing that got you to this place and you want it to get better. I am sure you are like most change agents in business in that you know that it takes a real leader to implement something new and make things better. I appreciate your drive for the growth of your people and I am excited about being a part of that growth. Our Leadership Mastery program seems to fit with what you indicated your needs and desires are. It makes sense to me to move forward and I would like to begin helping you as soon as I can. What do you need from me in order to move forward?

The Move is not complicated! It is about fulfilling the wants and needs of your prospect. If that is your focus, you will only allow them to buy what will actually accomplish that.

THE DELIVERY

The Delivery - This is the component of the sale
where you provide the product or service that the
new client/customer has purchased. Never
underestimate the importance of the relationship at
this point. How you deliver your product or service
will determine whether or not you are able to
complete the next step in the process.

The objective of this phase of the selling process is to
prove to the customer that their choice to buy from
you was a good one. You want them to witness the
expertise that they imagined in you when they signed
the agreement. Your goal...results!!! If you are a
trainer, like I am, then you need to really impress
them with your knowledge and delivery of the
information. If you are an accountant, then you need
to "wow" them with your ability to understand the tax
code and help them leverage their hard work. If you
are a mechanic, then you need to impress them with
your capacity for enhancing their vehicle's
engine. Whatever you are, this is your time to shine!

A few things that you need to keep in mind as you
deliver what you have sold the client...

1. Make sure that you are delivering what is in
   the proposal plus 1. The plus 1 is going one

step beyond what you promised. It is the plus 1 that, in my experience, really impresses clients the most. Don't stray away from what you committed to deliver. You simply want to deliver everything that was promised and a little more.

2. Your customer is your reason for existence. They are not a hindrance to your day, a slow-down to your work, or an interference in any way. They are the reason that you are in existence! Treat them as if they are the most important thing in your business life at that moment, because they are.

3. They must be more than happy! You have to continuously be uncovering what they want, how they feel, and how they are interpreting their experience with you. The sales process never ends. Don't focus on up-selling them on more products or services as you deliver what they bought. Focus on up-selling their image of you and the organization so that they will desire more from you.

Your ability to solidify your reputation by proving yourself is critical. Without this ability, you will not be able to move to step 6. And trust me, you want to be able to move to step 6.

THE RE-BUY

One of the lessons that I learned the hard way as a new entrepreneur was that it is much easier to get a current client to buy more from me than it is to get a new client to buy for the first time. It was this lesson that has made the biggest difference in revenue growth for my company, though. You see, there are two sells that are made with any customer.

The first sale is for them to buy the kind of product or service that you have to offer. The second sale is for them to buy it from you. Once you have made both of those sales, making them again should be easier than before.

Think for a minute about why you go back to the same person to buy a car, or furniture. You may even have a preference for whom you do your banking with. What does that interaction look like? What do they say and what do you say that makes you feel welcomed and valued? It is the emotional connection that creates the opportunity to serve that customer or client again. Your job, once you have a client, is to make sure that you exceed their expectations in the delivery of what they purchased.

One example of this was the sound board that I recently purchased for my church. As silly as it may sound, they included a small bag of assorted candy in the shipment of the digital mixer. It made me smile. Candy doesn't actually have anything to do with good music, or does it? It has to do with an emotional state that Sweetwater.com wanted me to have.

The day that the board was delivered, Ryan called me to make sure that I knew it was delivered. He then called me on Monday, after the first Sunday that we had the board hooked up. He made me feel that they cared. He wanted me to be satisfied with my board and how it all worked. He even sent me some links to video tutorials on the board. The net result... We have already purchased more from Sweetwater.

I began to look for ways to buy from them instead of just purchasing off of other websites. I did this because they delivered. All you have to do is the same. You must deliver. If you do, your customers will think of you first when they need something.

THE REFERRAL

The referral is not as tricky as you might think. Many times, people will work hard, do a good job, and then stand there looking at the person, hoping that they will magically think to tell others how happy they are. It is an unfortunate reality that there are lots of people who simply don't think to tell others, even when they are happy. As a trainer and speaker, one of the tactics that has made the biggest difference for me is to end my speeches and trainings with a statement. Here is that statement...

If you have enjoyed this program, I would ask that you tell everyone that you have ever met. Post on Facebook about it. Tell your friends on LinkedIn. You can even personally pay for a billboard on the interstate. That seems a little excessive to me, but I am alright with it. If you didn't enjoy it or didn't get what you had hoped for, please tell me. I want to make sure that my programs are better and better each time.

Right as I say the last statement, I smile really big and gesture in a large bow. This lets people know that we are truly finished at this point and they are free to go.

Since I added that statement as the conclusion to my programs, my referrals have gone up 10-fold. I get 10 times as many referrals as I got before that. The objective is to make it a little fun to give a referral and to plant in their mind that you would like the referrals. By asking them to post on social media, many of them actually do. They tell their friends that they were trained by me and therefore plant the idea of hiring me in the minds of their friends.

Never be afraid to ask for a referral if you have done your very best and have helped your client or customer to achieve the results they desire. If you are selling with honor, then you deserve a great referral!

ABOUT THE AUTHOR

Jody Holland is an author, trainer, speaker, coach, and sales warrior. Jody has been in sales for more than 3 decades in one form or another. He has done inside sales, outside sales, professional service sales, recruiting, and fundraising. His capacity for inspiring others to take action that is good for them and for their organization has created opportunity after opportunity.

Jody is married and has two beautiful daughters. He strives to live his life in such a way that others will see that he has a code of honor that guides him. Jody has written 18 other books, all of which can be found on Amazon.com/author/jodyholland

Book Title	Subject
My Judo Life	Turning Life's Challenges Into Opportunities
The Quest	Finding Purpose In Life
Living The Quest	Applying the 8 Lessons From The Quest
25 Activities In A Bag	Teambuilding Anywhere
Turn Me On	How To Give Great Presentations
Just Make Time	Prioritizing Your Life and Winning Without Wearing Out
Leadership Evo	The 4 Styles of Leadership and How To Succeed As A Business Leader
Breakthrough Leadership	How To Break Through Barriers and Inspire Others To Do The Same
Success – A 12 Step Program	The 12 Steps To Living A Success In Life
The 12 Principles of Success	12 Principles Successful People Live By
A Life of Miracles	A 60-Day Journey To Reshape Your Thoughts On Reality
Psyche of Success – Volume 1	A Collection Of Wisdom From Great Speakers and Leaders
Hypnotic Selling	How To Use NLP, Conversational Hypnosis, and Face Reading To Increase Your Sales
Yay! I'm A Supervisor! Now What?! (Also In Spanish)	The 12 Key Skills Great Leaders Must Master In Order To Succeed With People
6 Demons of Fear	How To Overcome The 6 Human Fears That Hold Us Back (Parable)
Smart. A.S.S. (Accelerated Success System)	The Secret Psychology of Winning Big in Business And in Life
#GSD Planner	Get Stuff Done Planner that helps you map out targets, wins, schedules, and dreams, while keeping your focus on what matters
Success Journal	A Journal For Tracking Your Days, Thoughts, Challenges, and Life

Made in the USA
Columbia, SC
27 June 2023

19342685R00061